COLOR YOUR OWN WALL ART

Botanicals

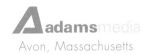

Aadamsmedia

Avon, Massachusetts

Published by
Adams Media, a division of F+W Media, Inc.
57 Littlefield Street, Avon, MA 02322. U.S.A.
www.adamsmedia.com

Contains material adapted from *Instant Wall Art: Botanical Prints*, copyright © 2015 by F+W Media,
Inc., ISBN 10: 1-4405-8566-0, ISBN 13: 978-1-4405-8566-1.

ISBN 10: 1-5072-0034-X
ISBN 13: 978-1-5072-0034-6

Printed in the United States of America.

10 9 8 7 6 5 4 3 2 1

Cover design by Sylvia McArdle.
Cover and interior illustrations by Claudia Wolf.

This book is available at quantity discounts for bulk purchases.
For information, please call 1-800-289-0963.

COLOR YOUR OWN WALL ART

Botanicals

25 Color-By-Number Designs

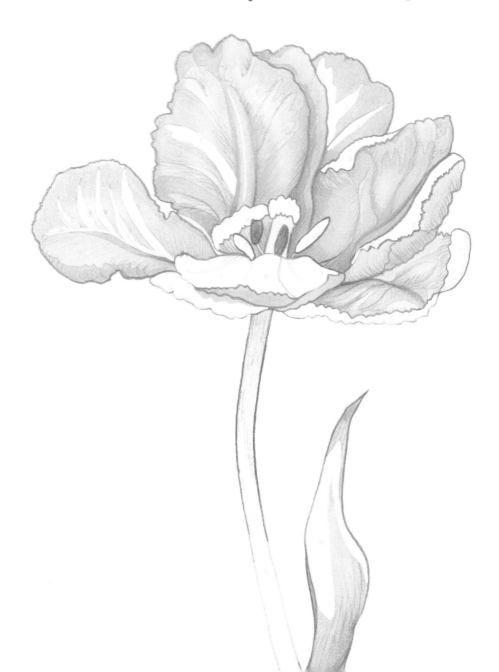

Introduction

Today, beautiful botanical prints are showing up everywhere you look—from popular design magazines and websites to the walls of your friends' living rooms and kitchens.

And now, instead of having to choose between one or two expensive prints, you can choose from the twenty-five stylish illustrations found within the pages of *Color Your Own Wall Art Botanicals* to create customized artwork for your walls. It's the perfect way to decorate your space with the latest trend and show off your artistic side at the same time.

From lush peonies to feathery ferns to flowering cacti, you're sure to find a print that is perfect for your walls. The best part is, each illustration has been numbered so you can flawlessly add color to bring the plants to life.

Refer to the color palette on the inside cover of this book to find the color that corresponds with each number. Any spaces that aren't numbered should remain white. You'll also find a fully colored version of each image on the inside of the front or back cover to give you a preview of the lovely picture you will create when you follow the number pattern exactly. But if you'd rather, let your own unique palette guide your hand and personalize your image to match your individual style.

Use the test pages in this book to check your colors and practice your application techniques. Have fun and experiment with the amount of pressure you use as you color. Practice transitioning from heavy pressure to light pressure to create a blended look that adds depth and re-creates the look of sunlight on the plants.

- Using heavy pressure will create stronger color saturation and can help create the appearance of a shadow.

- Light pressure will create less color saturation and can help create the appearance of a highlight.

- The numbers will help you determine exactly where to place shadows (darker colors) and highlights (lighter colors). Use more pressure at the edge of a darker section and gradually reduce your pressure as you move toward a lighter section.

- Refer to the full colored version of your image as you color for further help in placing the shadows and highlights.

These botanical prints measure 8" x 10" and will fit in a standard mat and frame once removed from the book at the perforated edge. So choose the prints you love, color them, and hang them on your walls to enjoy the beauty of nature, and your own creativity, year-round!

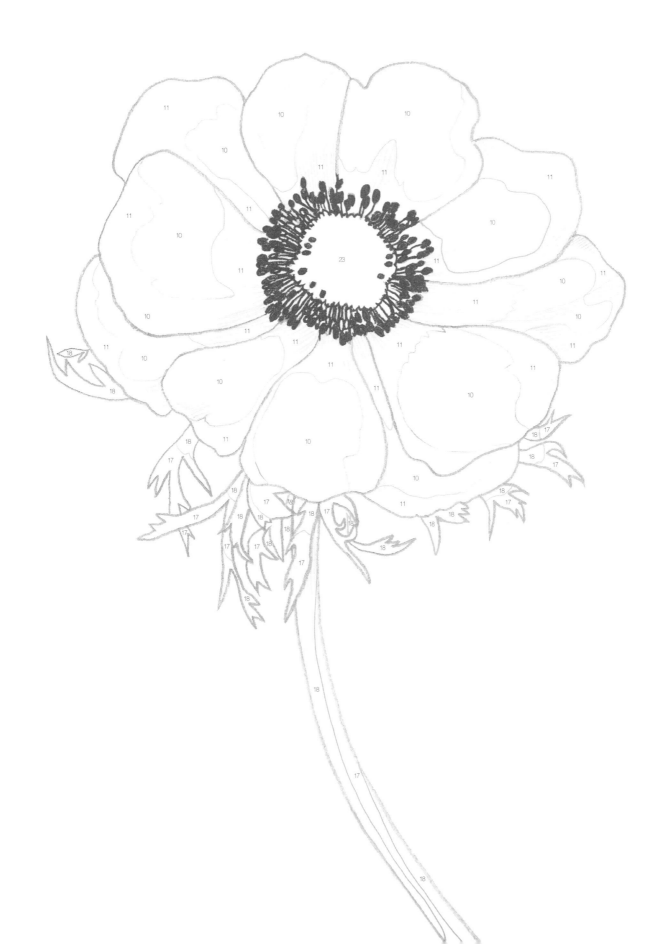

FLOWER 1

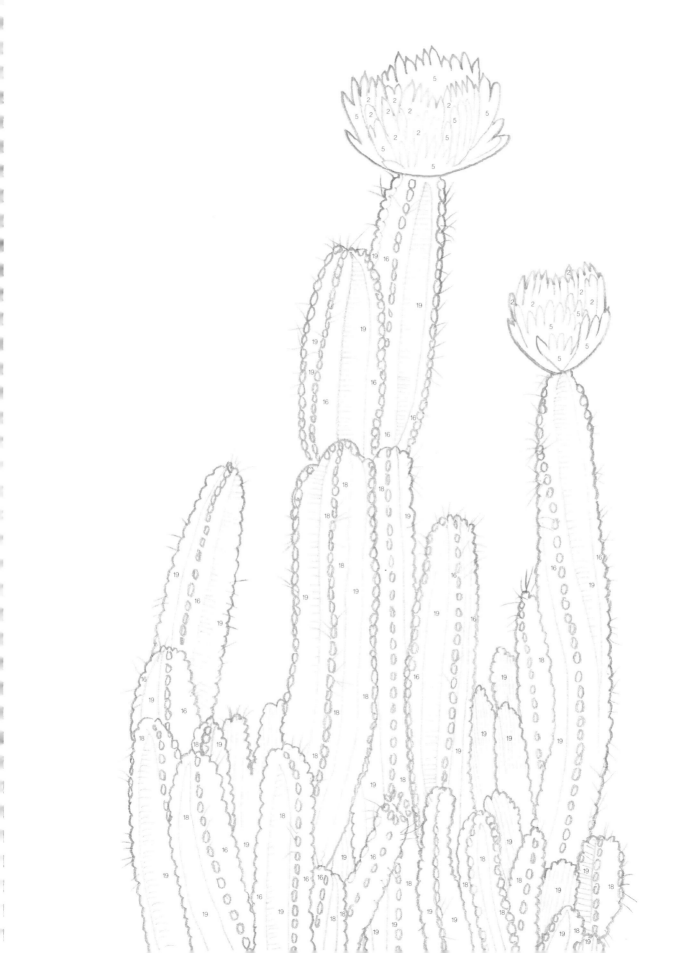

FLOWER 2

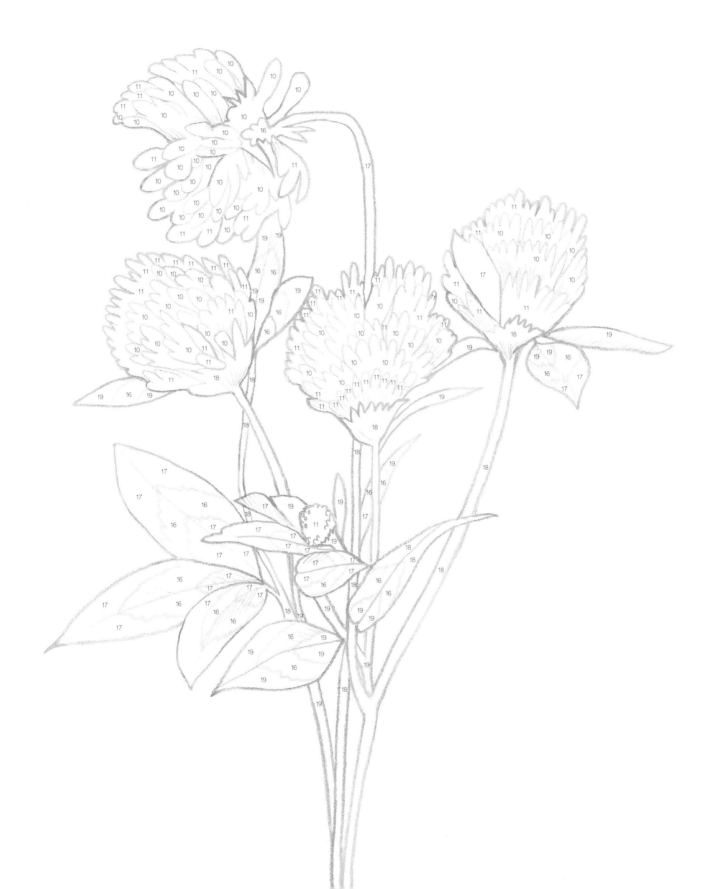

FLOWER 3

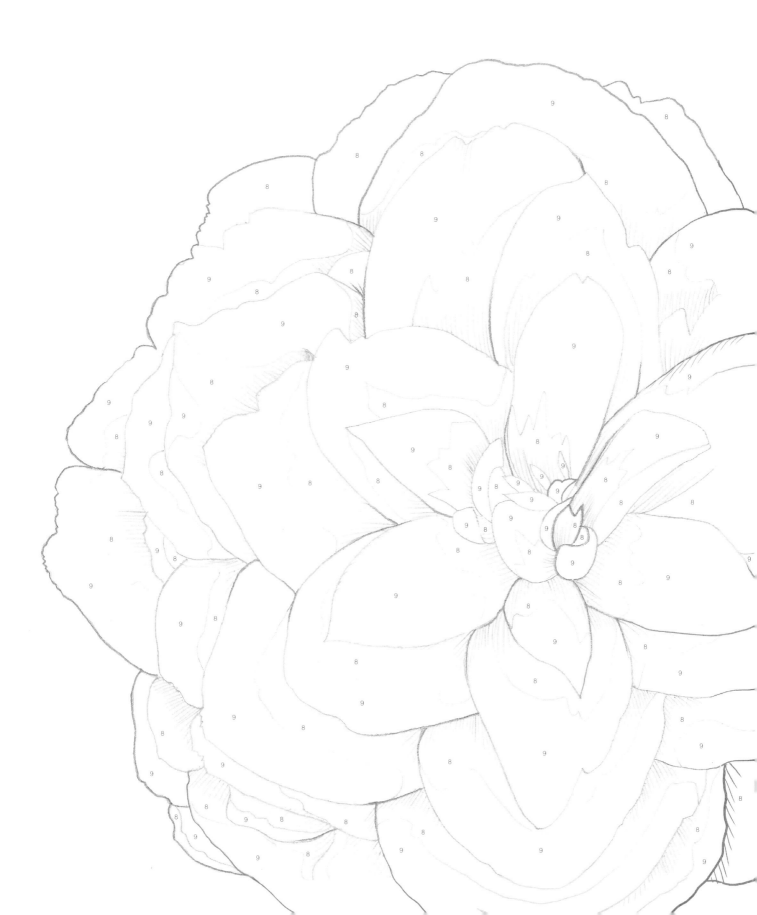

FLOWER 4

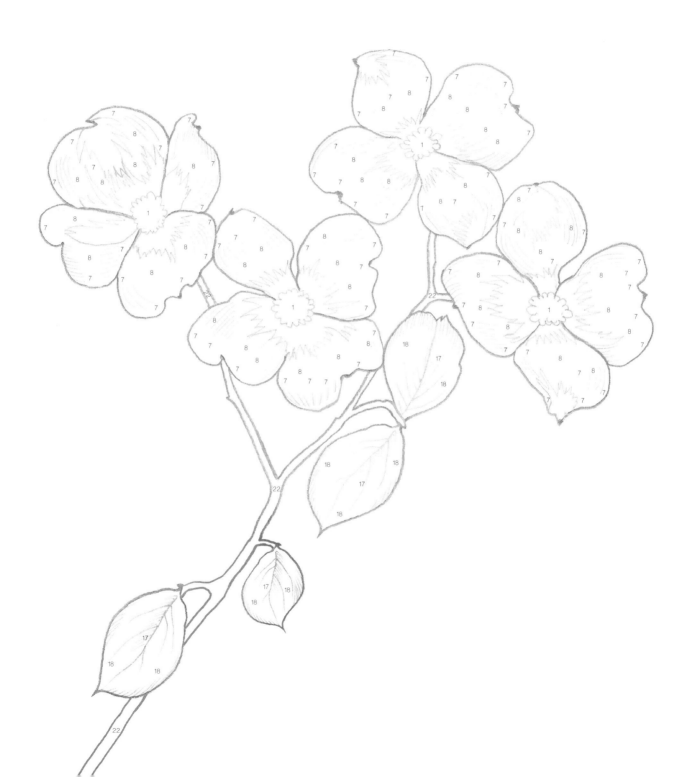

FLOWER 5

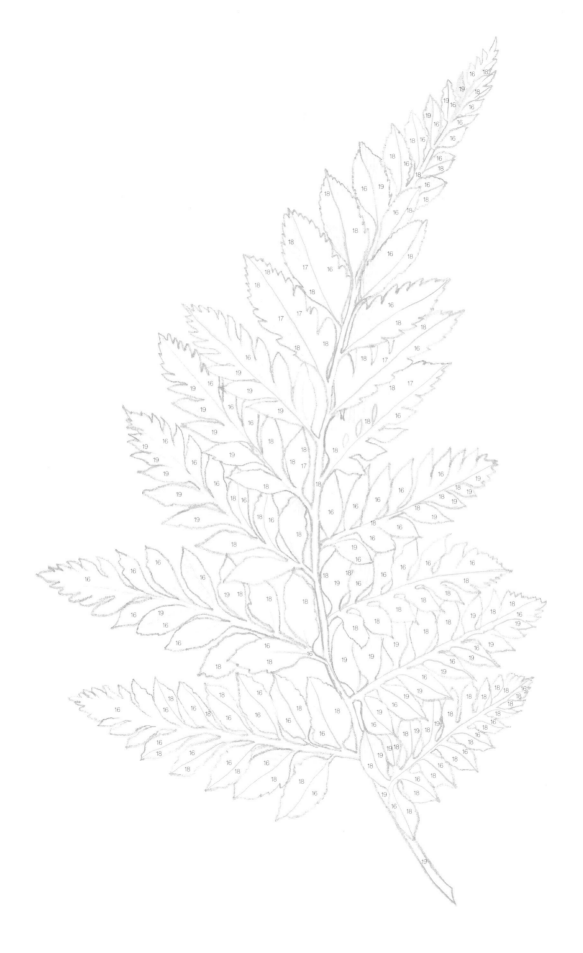

FLOWER 6

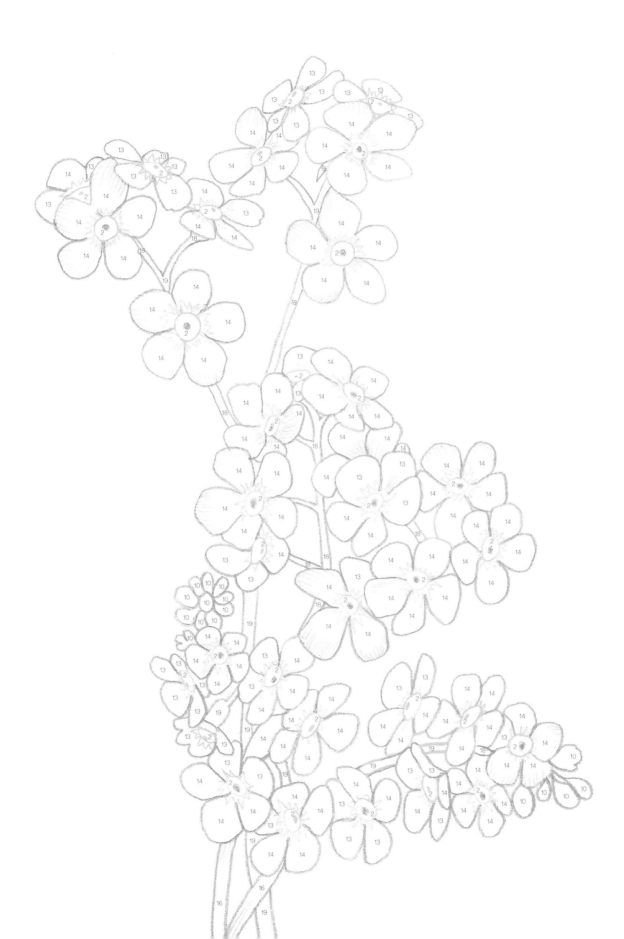

FLOWER 7

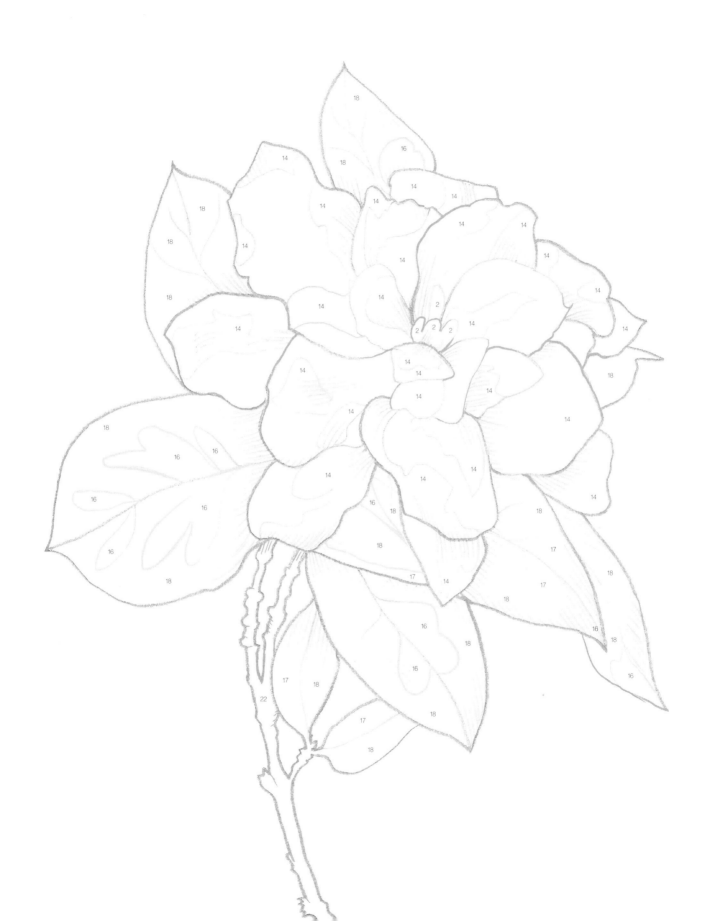

FLOWER 8

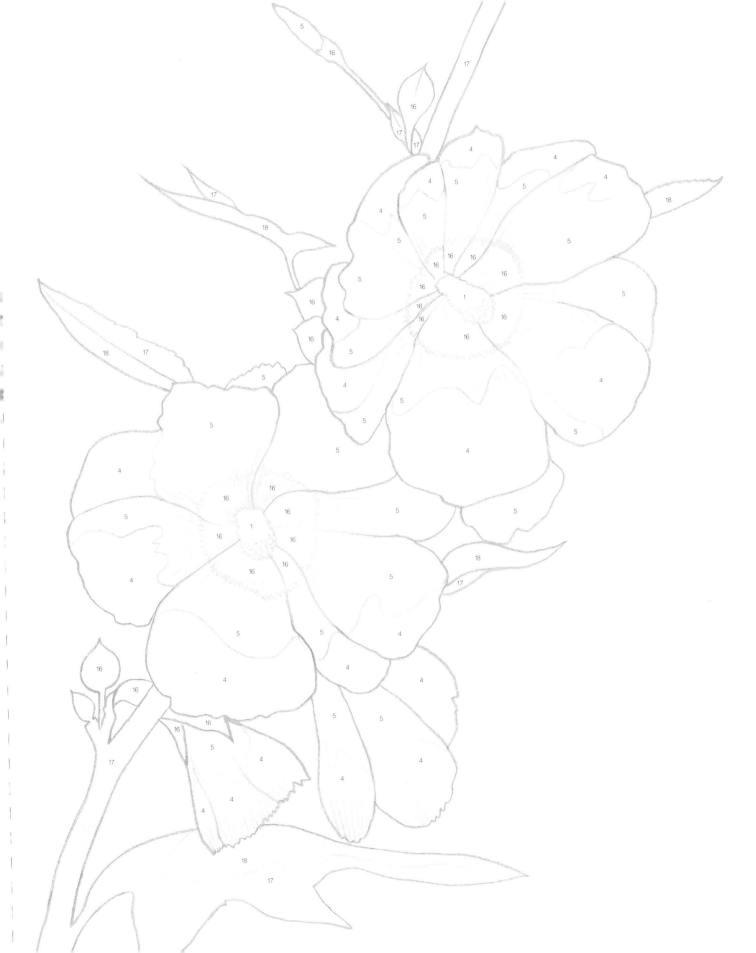

FLOWER 9

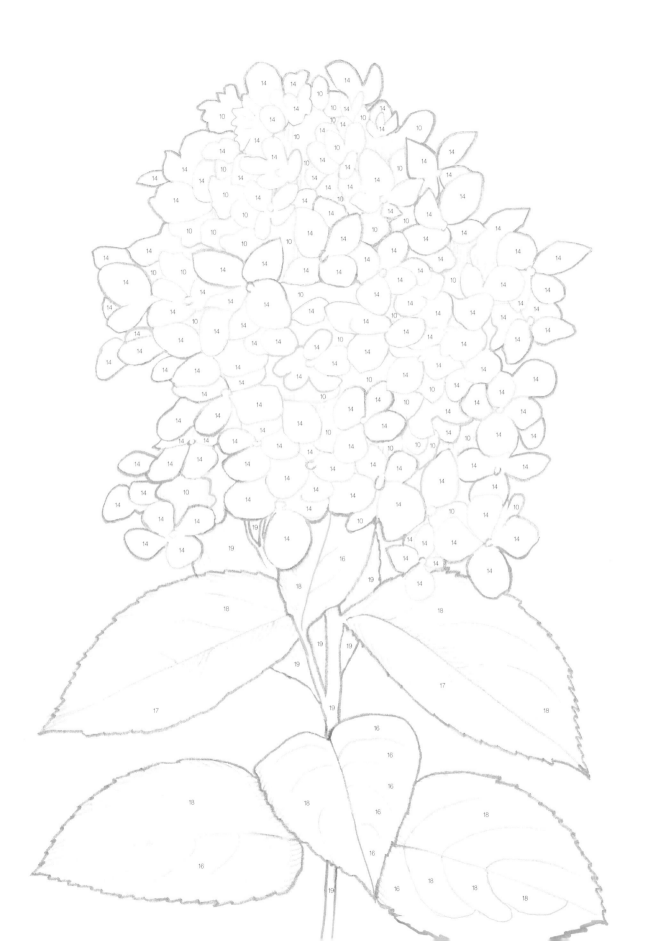

FLOWER 10

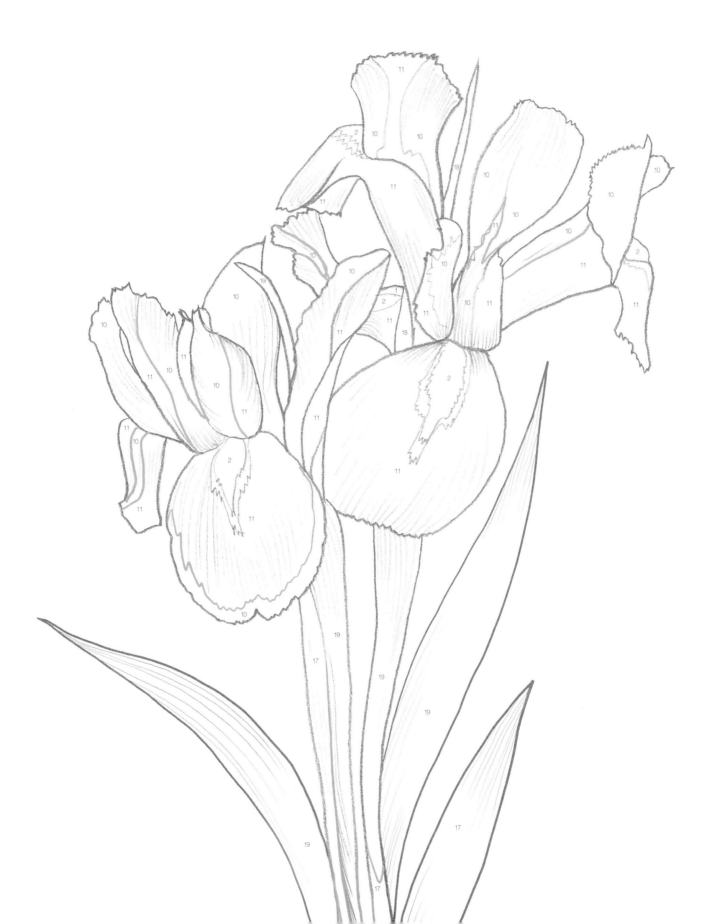

FLOWER 11

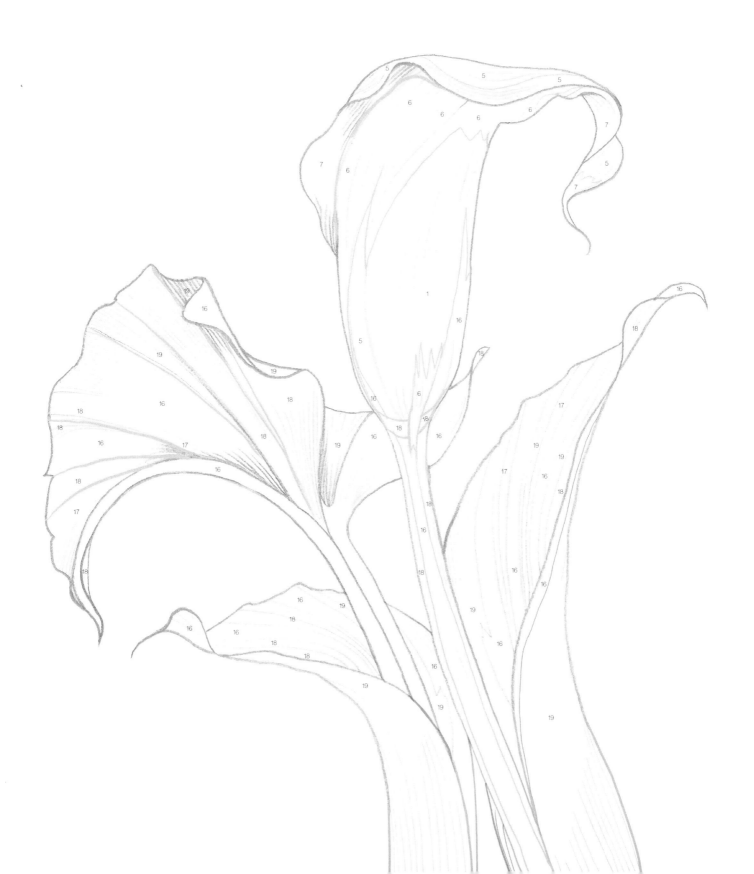

FLOWER 12

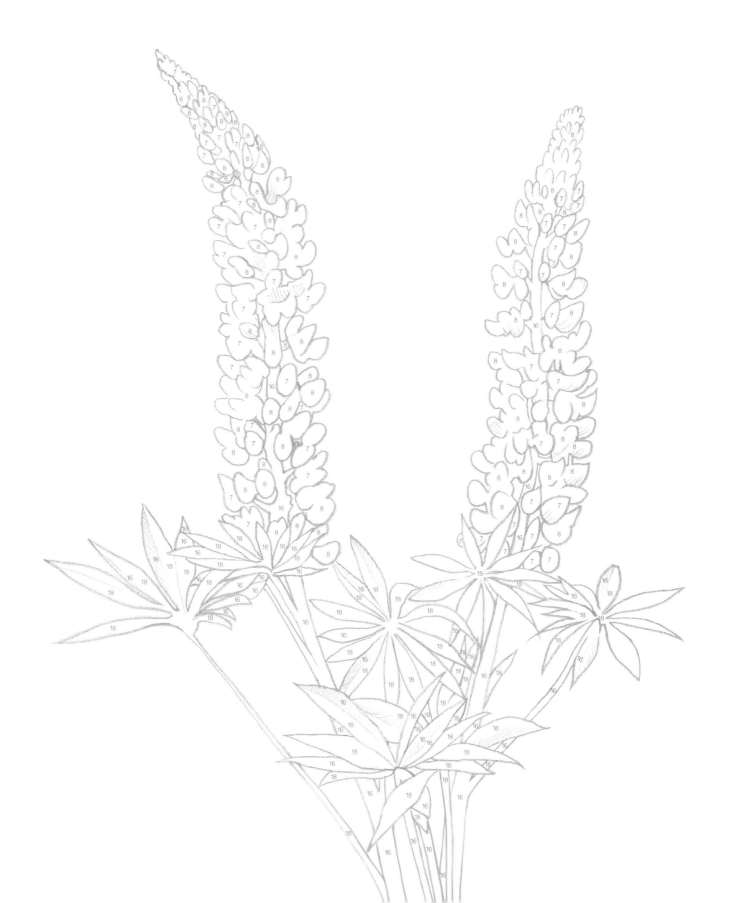

FLOWER 13

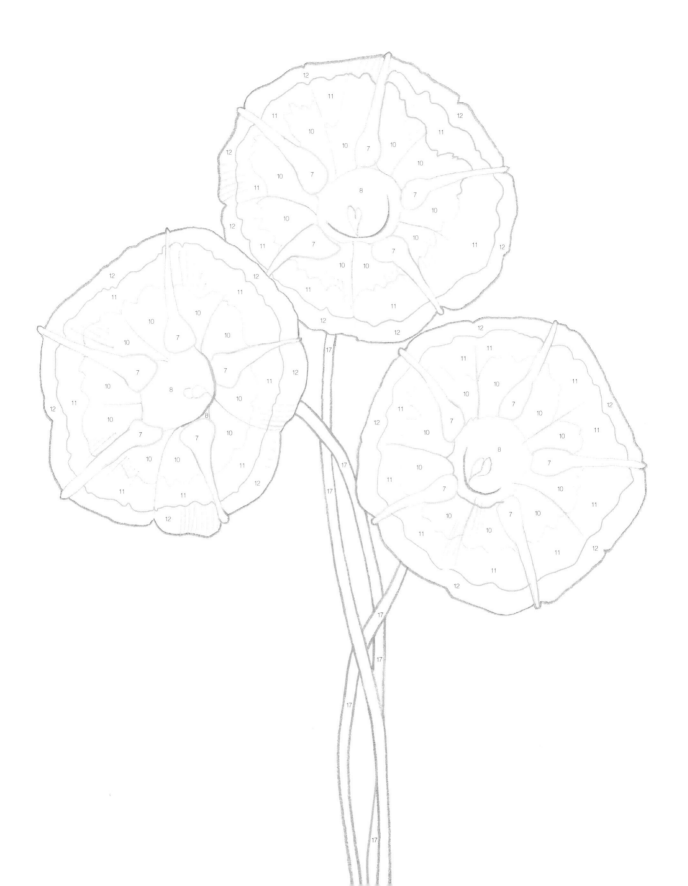

FLOWER 14

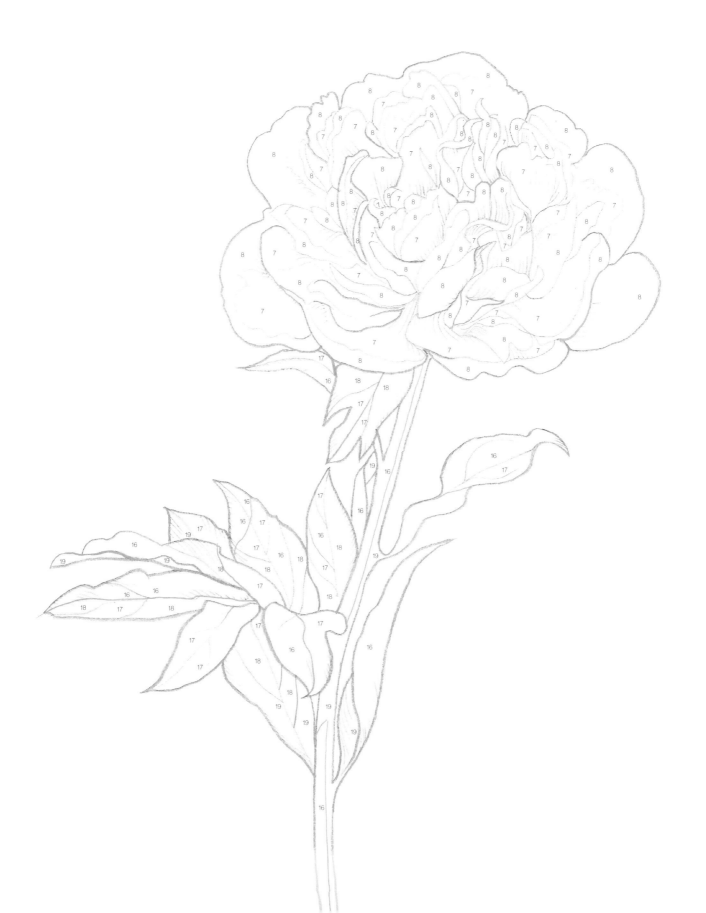

FLOWER 15

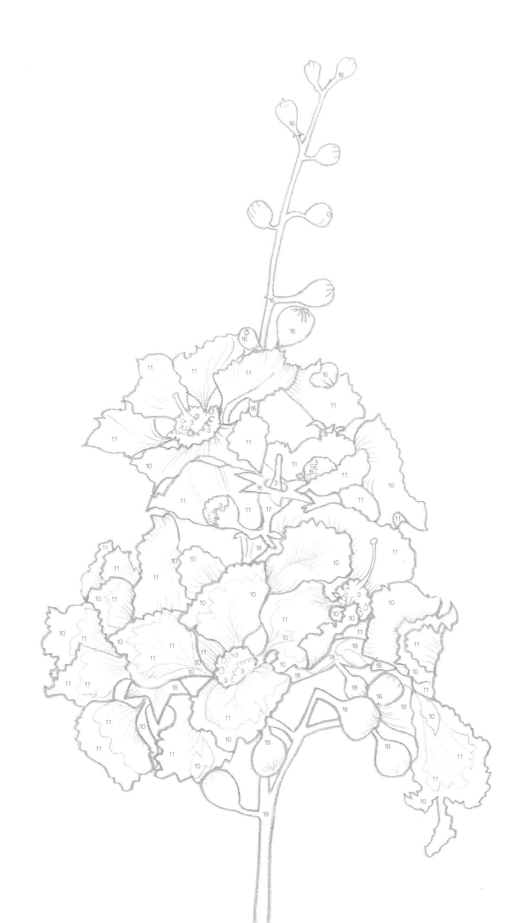

FLOWER 16

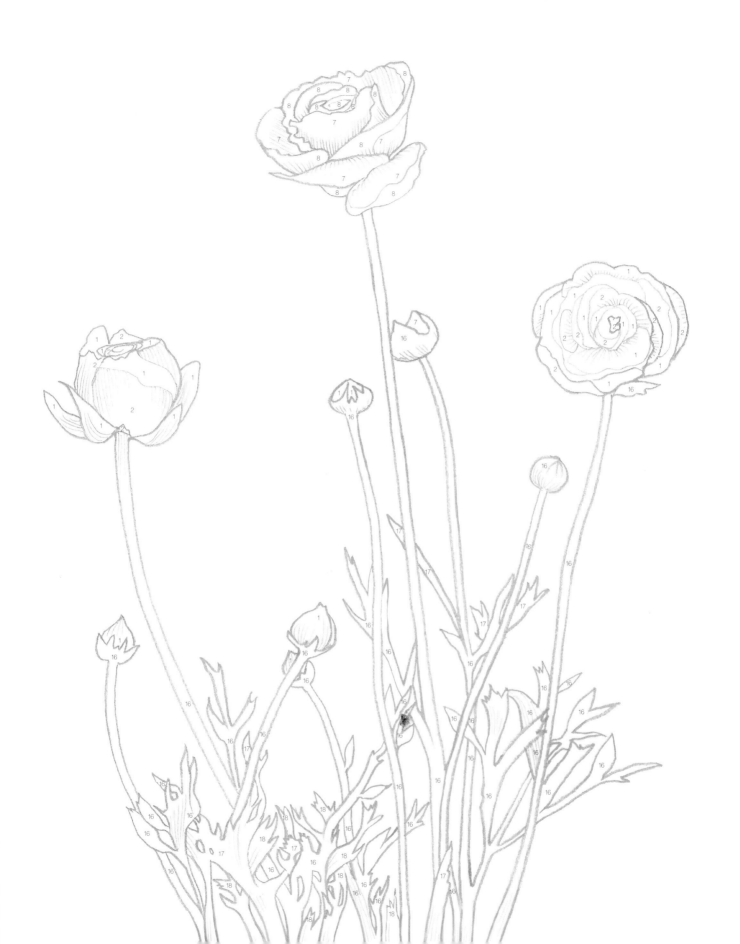

FLOWER 17

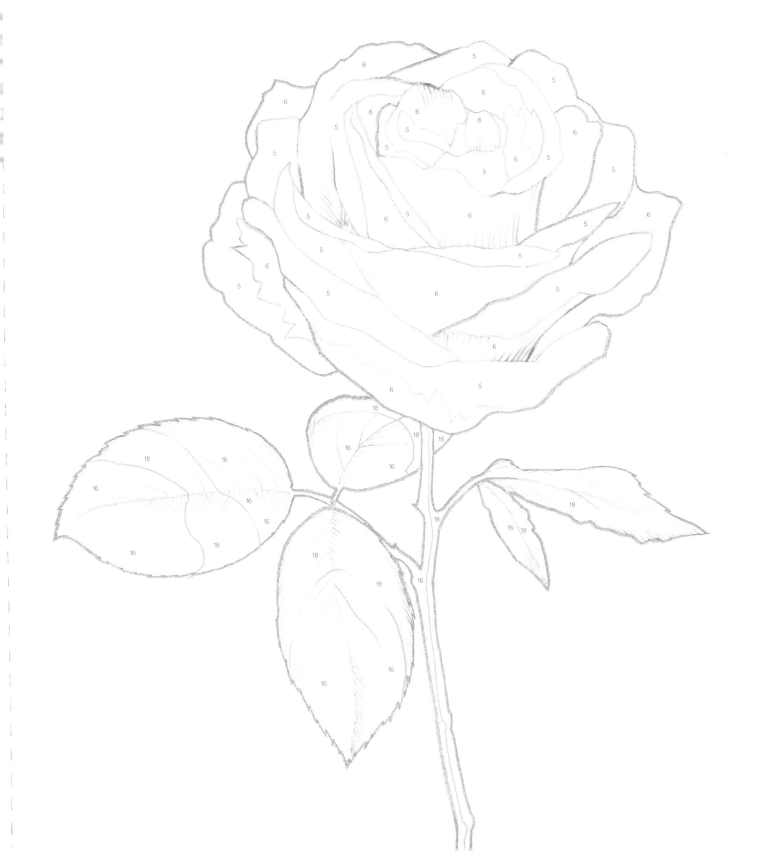

FLOWER 18

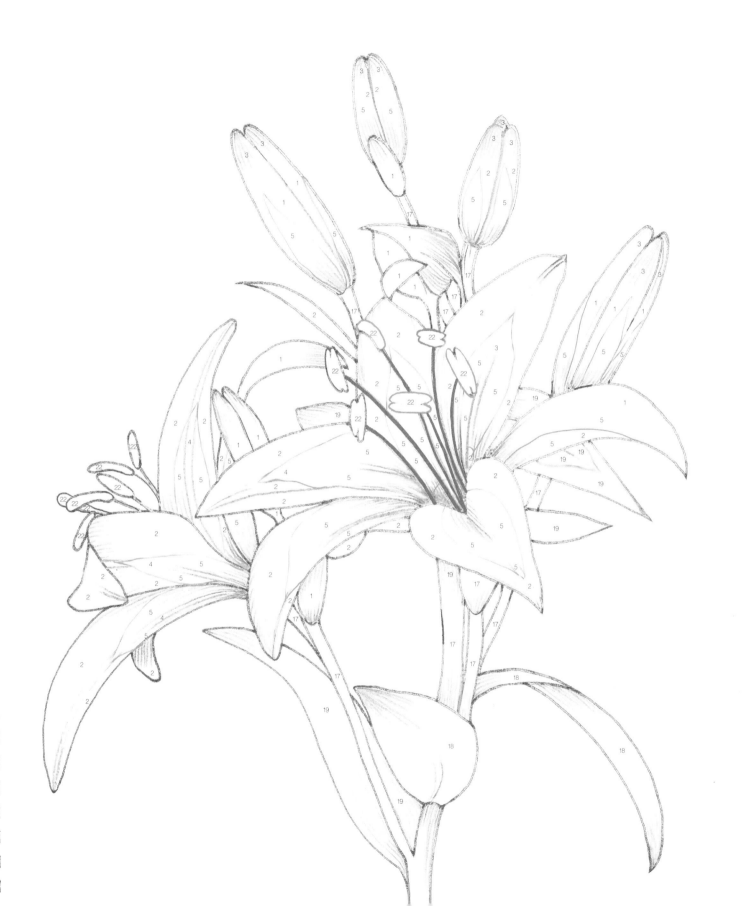

FLOWER 19

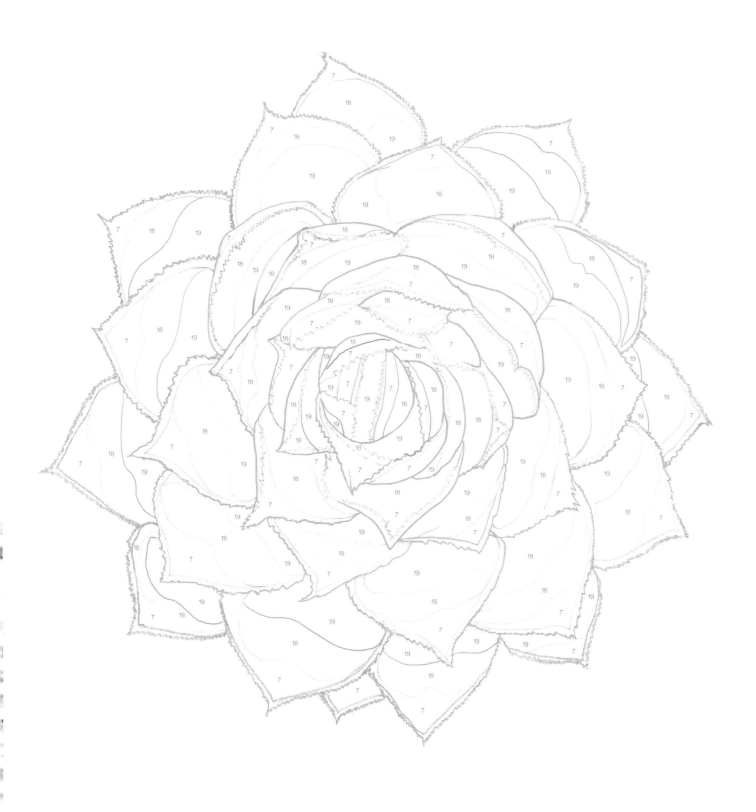

FLOWER 20

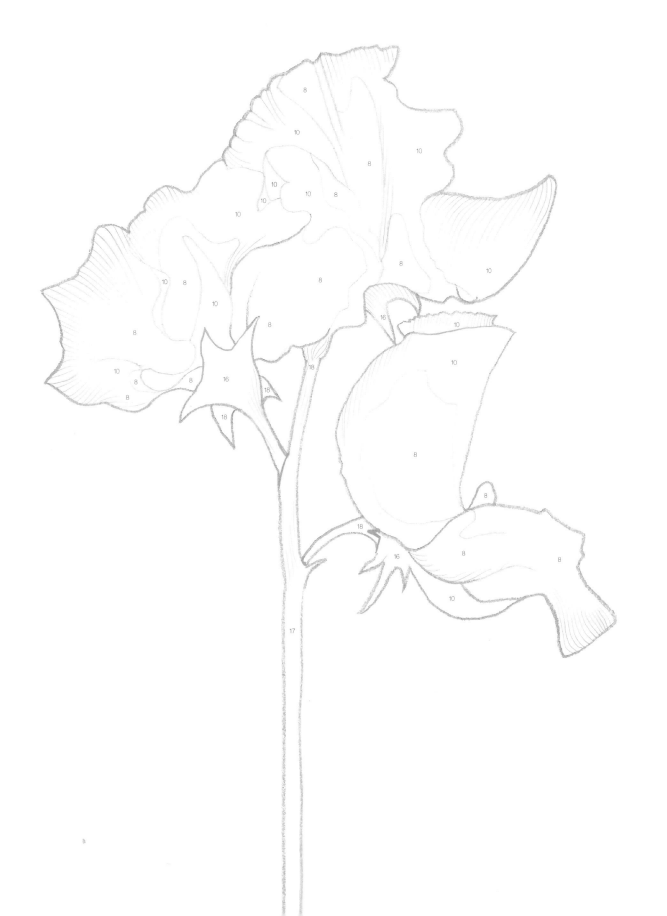

FLOWER 21

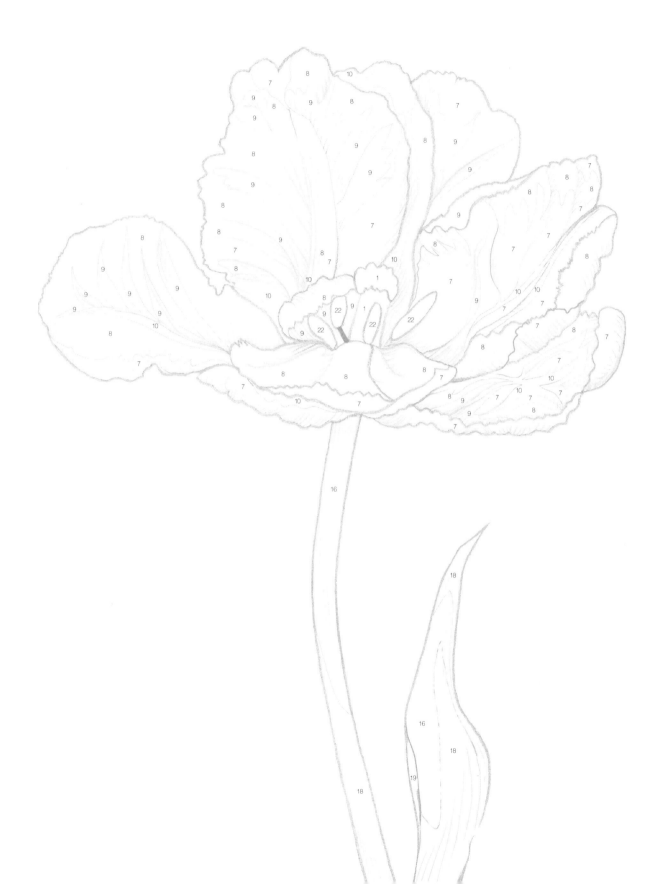

FLOWER 22

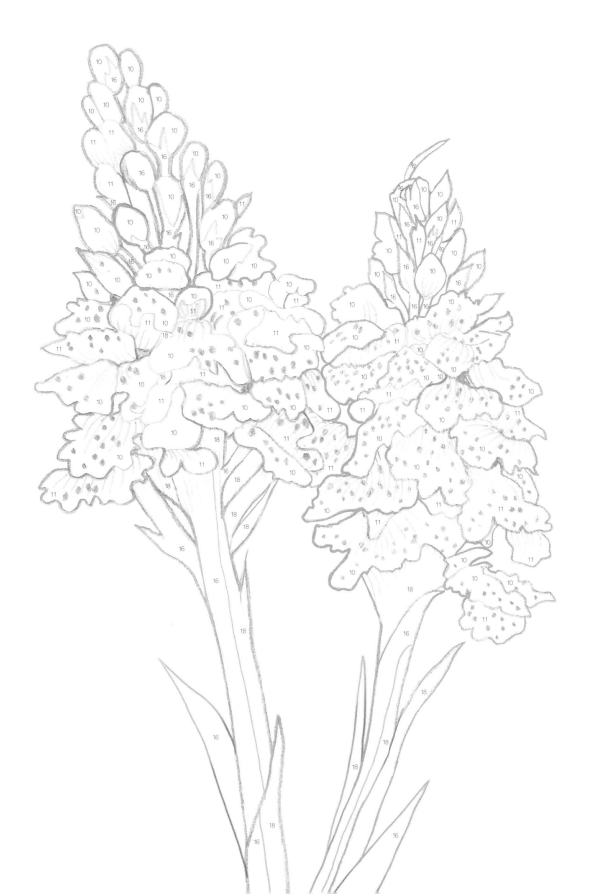

FLOWER 23

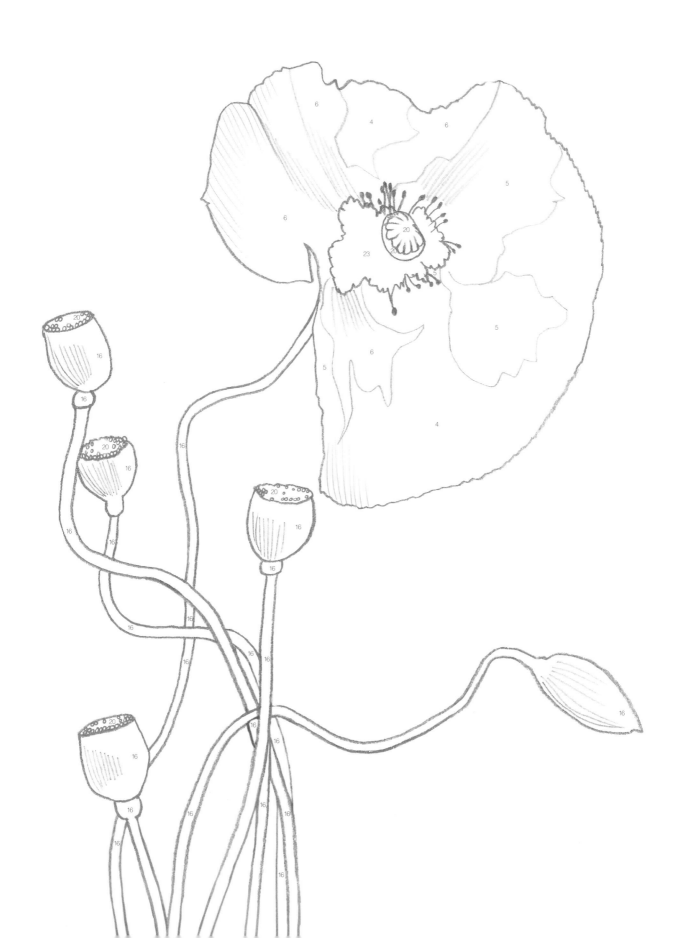

FLOWER 24

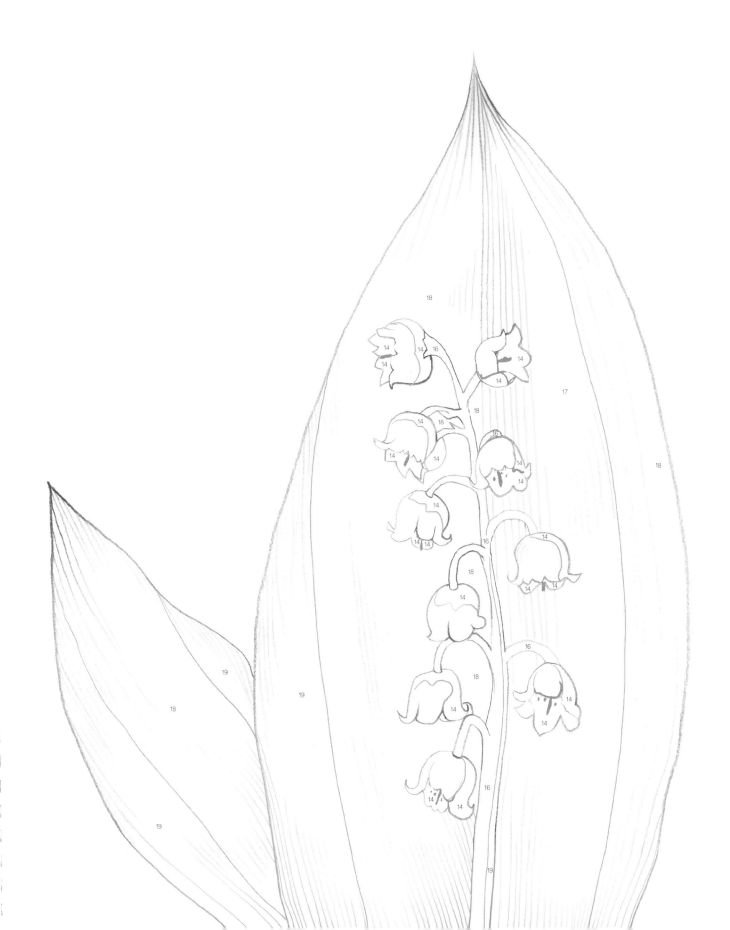

FLOWER 25

TEST PAGES